blue zoo guides

ocean life

by Dee Phillips and
Alison Howard

™

MINNETONKA, MINNESOTA

Published in North America in 2006 by Two-Can Publishing
11571 K-Tel Drive, Minnetonka, MN 55343
www.two-canpublishing.com

Copyright © ticktock Entertainment Ltd 2006
First published in Great Britain in 2006 by ticktock Media Ltd.,
Unit 2, Orchard Business Centre, North Farm Road, Tunbridge Wells, Kent, TN2 3XF

Library of Congress Cataloging-in-Publication Data

Phillips, Dee, 1967–

Ocean life / by Dee Phillips and Alison Howard.

p. cm. — (Blue zoo guides)

Includes index.

Summary: "Introduces a number of ocean creatures from around the world, including fish, mammals, reptiles, birds, and invertebrates. Includes information about where in the ocean they live, what they eat, and how they grow and survive"—Provided by publisher.

ISBN 1-58728-560-6 (reinforced hardcover)

1. Marine animals—Juvenile literature. I. Howard, Alison (Alison Jane), 1954– II. Title. III. Series.

QL122.2.P477 2006

591.77--dc22

2006013267

Picture Credits: Alamy; 81, FLPA; P11, 23, 38t. OSF; 39, 40t, 41, 61.

1 2 3 4 5 10 09 08 07 06

Printed in China

Contents

Words that appear in **bold** are explained in the glossary.

Meet the
Ocean Creatures

The oceans are home to fascinating creatures of all shapes and sizes. Many of them live near the ocean's surface, where sunlight warms the water and plants can grow. Others have special skills that allow them to survive thousands of feet below the surface, in complete darkness and extreme cold. This book will introduce you to a bunch of these cool ocean critters. But before you turn the page, here's some helpful information on the different groups of animals that you'll meet.

Fish

Fish are **vertebrates**—the name for all animals that have a backbone. Fish live their entire lives in water, using **gills** to breathe. Their bodies are covered in flat, slippery **scales.**

Birds

Birds are vertebrates. They have wings, feathers, and a light but strong skeleton. Most birds are excellent fliers. Baby birds hatch from eggs.

Invertebrates

Invertebrates are animals that do not have a backbone. Some have a tough covering (such as a shell or skin) that protects their soft insides. This group includes ocean animals such as lobsters, oysters, and starfish.

Mammals

Mammals are vertebrates, too. Mammal moms feed their babies with their own milk, and most give birth to live young. Ocean mammals must come to the surface to breathe air.

Reptiles

Reptiles are vertebrates that have tough skin made of scales. Most reptiles, including those that live mainly in water, lay eggs on land. Other reptiles give birth to live young.

A Watery World

The map on this page shows our world.

See all the blue areas? They are oceans, and they cover more than half of the earth's surface. The other colors show areas of land called continents. North America and Africa are continents.

Some of the animals you'll meet in this book live in oceans all over the world, while others are found only in certain areas.

When you read about an animal in this book, see if you can find the place where it lives on the map. Can you find where YOU live?

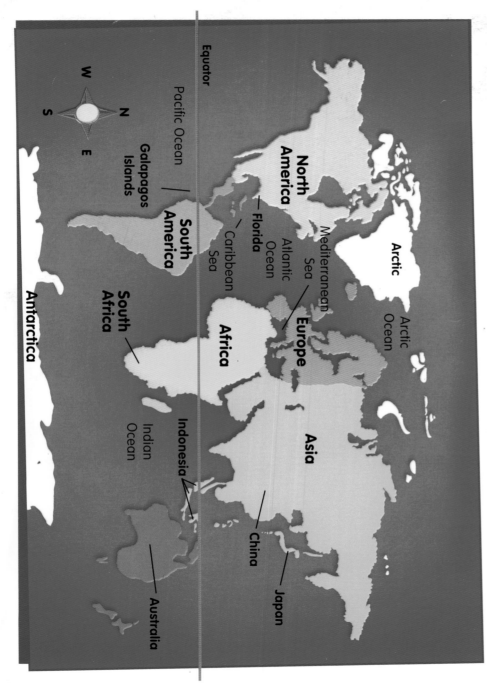

Ocean Habitats

The ocean may seem like one giant pool of salty water, but it's not. Oceans at the top and bottom of the earth are called polar regions, and they are icy cold. Oceans near the equator (an invisible line around the middle of the earth) are warm year round. The ocean's surface, shallow areas, and shorelines sparkle in the sun, while deep **seabeds** are dark and chilly.

These different areas of the ocean are called habitats. And each habitat is home to ocean animals that are perfectly suited to life there. Look for these pictures in your book, and they will tell you what kind of habitat each ocean creature lives in.

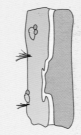

Seashore – the shallow salty water and rocky or sandy areas where oceans meet land

Polar regions – cold frozen places at the very top and bottom of the earth

Oceans – huge open areas of deep, salty water

Seabed – the bottom of the ocean

Tropical waters – warm waters near the equator

Anglerfish

The anglerfish lives in the Mediterranean Sea and the Pacific and Atlantic Oceans. Females have a long fin that looks like a fishing rod.

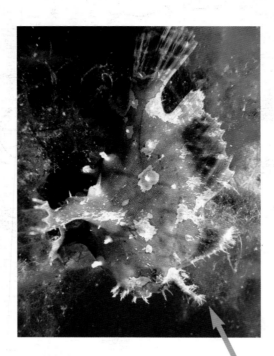

Anglerfish sit on the seabed and wait for their next meal to swim by. They eat other fish.

Anglerfish have a long fin that looks like a fishing rod.

Like all fish, the anglerfish has gills for breathing. In this picture, the gills are the red lines you can see in the fish's mouth.

How **BIG** is an **anglerfish**?

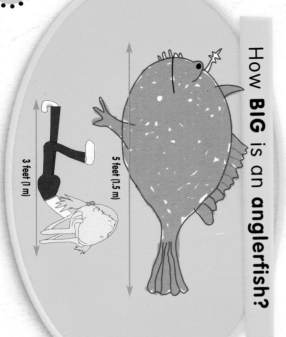

5 feet (1.5 m)

3 feet (1 m)

Anglerfish eggs float up to the surface of the water, where they hatch.

Soon after hatching, a male anglerfish may find a female anglerfish and attach himself to her belly. Then he knows right where to find a mate when it's time to **breed.**

Hatchetfish

Hatchetfish are found in oceans around the world, but mainly in the western Pacific. There are about 45 known **species**, or kinds. The shape of their body looks a little like a hatchet, or ax.

Hatchetfish have silver sides that **reflect** light and make them almost invisible in the water.

Hatchetfish live in deep, dark waters, 1,500 to 2,000 feet (450 to 600 m) below the surface.

How **BIG** is a **hatchetfish?**

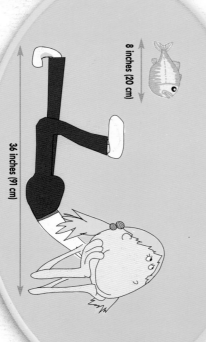

8 inches (20 cm)

36 inches (91 cm)

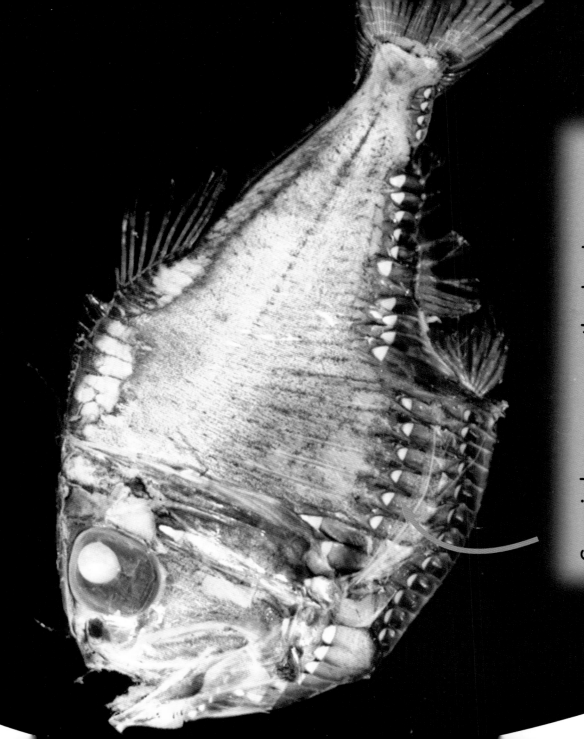

Hatchetfish feed during the day. They eat small fish, **crustaceans,** and the **fry** of larger fish.

Special organs on the body produce a dim light that confuses **predators** and also attracts **prey.**

Pufferfish

Most kinds of pufferfish live in warm, **tropical** seas. When they feel threatened, they gulp down water, which makes them puff up like a balloon.

Some pufferfish have spines that lie flat against their bodies. When the fish puffs up, these spines stick out so that predators have trouble biting it.

Pufferfish have powerful, beak-like snouts, which they use to crush their food.

How **BIG** is a **pufferfish?**

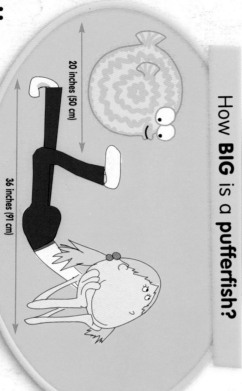

20 inches (50 cm)

36 inches (91 cm)

A pufferfish's body contains a poison that makes it unsafe to eat.

Pufferfish feed on **mollusks,** crustaceans, and coral (see page 86).

Clownfish

Clownfish are small, brightly colored fish. They live among the **tentacles** of sea anemones (see page 88) in tropical waters. A layer of slime on their bodies keeps them from getting stung.

Clownfish eat tiny ocean animals and **algae**. They also help out sea anemones by removing and eating tiny **parasites.**

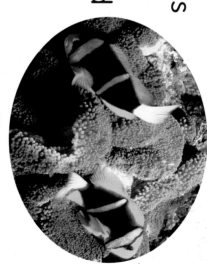

Clownfish get their name from their bright markings, which look like a clown's makeup.

How **BIG** is a **clownfish?**

5 inches (12 cm)

36 inches (91 cm)

Clownfish usually live in pairs within a sea anemone. They lay their eggs on nearby rocks.

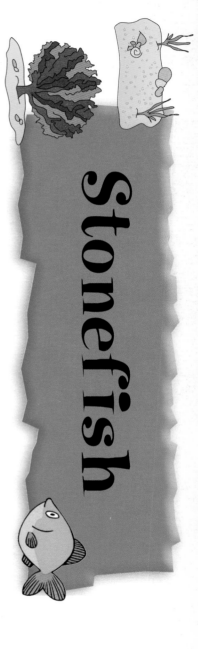

Stonefish

The stonefish lives in tropical waters. It has rough, patterned skin that makes it look just like a stone. This helps it to hide from predators and surprise its prey.

Stonefish have sharp spines on their backs that can squirt deadly **venom,** or poison, at an enemy.

A stonefish will not swim away from trouble. It will face any creature that tries to bother it.

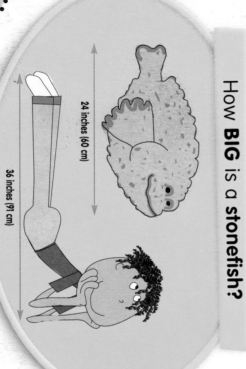

How **BIG** is a **stonefish?**

24 inches (60 cm)

36 inches (91 cm)

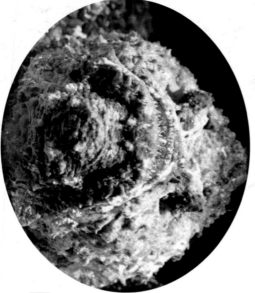

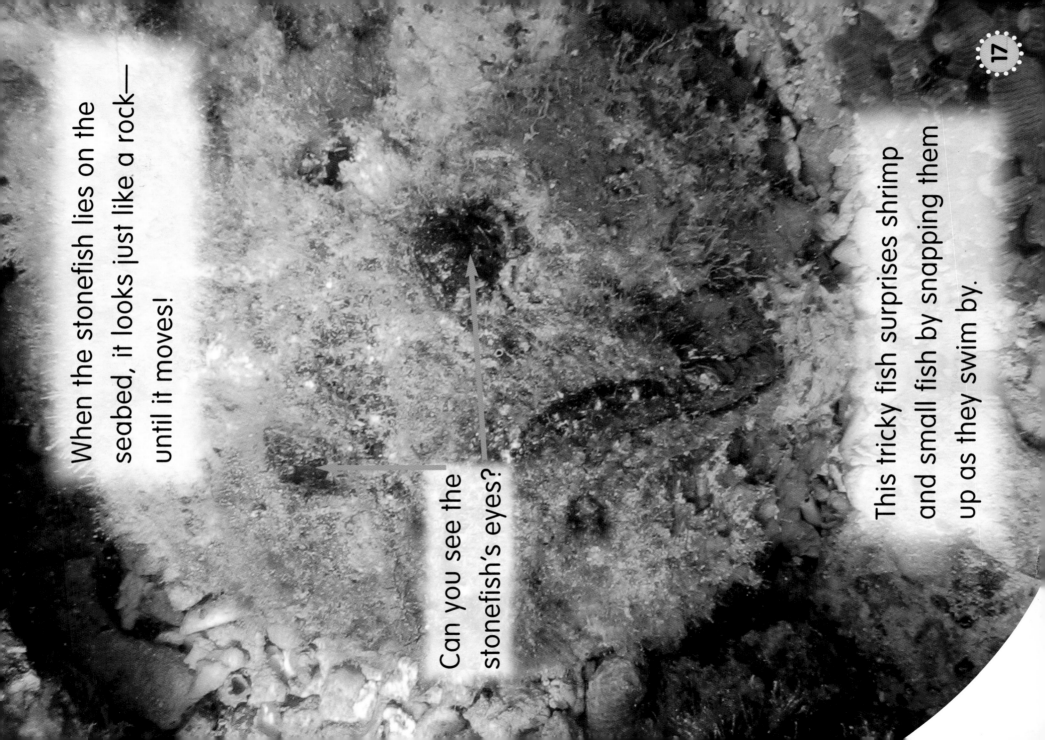

When the stonefish lies on the seabed, it looks just like a rock—until it moves!

Can you see the stonefish's eyes?

This tricky fish surprises shrimp and small fish by snapping them up as they swim by.

Coelacanth

The coelacanth (pronounced "SEE-la-canth") is an amazing and unusual fish that existed way back at the time of the dinosaurs. It is very rare and lives in oceans near South Africa and Indonesia.

People thought coelacanths were **extinct** until one was caught in 1938.

How **BIG** is a **coelacanth** ?

5 feet (1.5 m)

3 feet (1 m)

A coelacanth can open its mouth very wide. Its teeth are all in the front of its mouth.

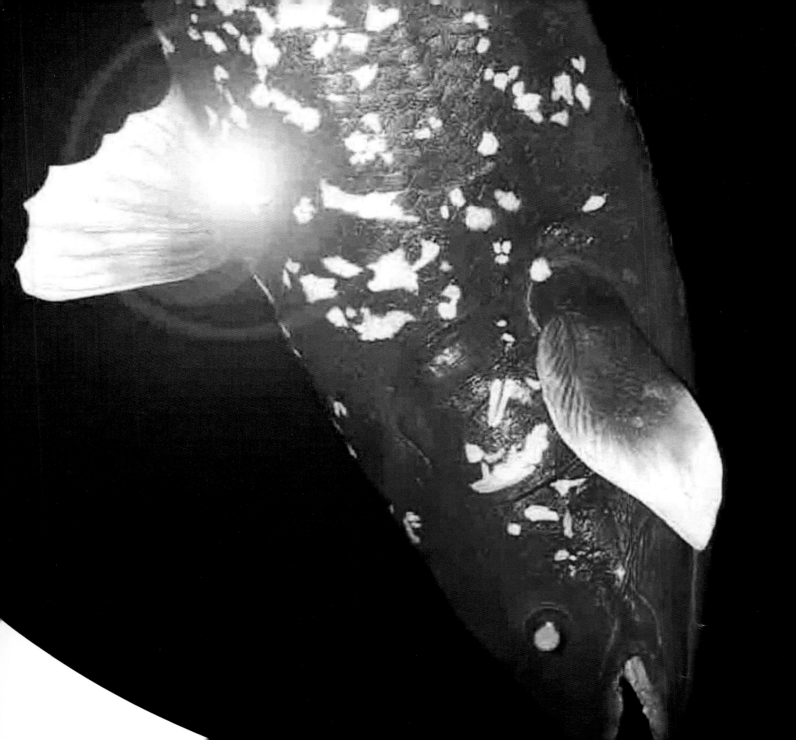

Unlike most other fish, which lay eggs, female coelacanths give birth to live babies.

Flounder

Flounder are a group of flat fish with patterned skin. They live in shallow waters and **estuaries** off the coasts of Europe and North America.

Flounder skim the seabed, eating small fish, squid, and shrimp.

This is a winter flounder.

A flounder is covered in prickly scales. It has a single, feathery fin that circles most of its body.

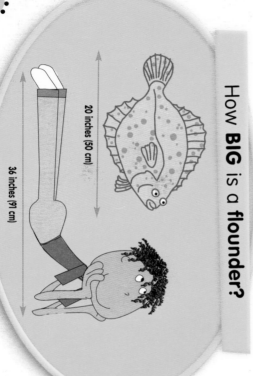

How **BIG** is a **flounder**?

20 inches (50 cm)

36 inches (91 cm)

Young flounder look like normal fish, with one eye on each side of the body. Gradually, their bodies flatten and both eyes move to the same side. This is a European flounder.

Atlantic Salmon

The Atlantic salmon is the best-known of many types of salmon. It is found in the northern Atlantic Ocean, but it swims up rivers to lay its eggs in shallow holes.

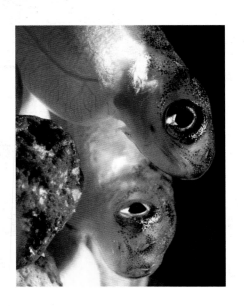

Female salmon lay their eggs in winter, and the males **fertilize** them. The babies hatch the following spring.

How **BIG** is an **Atlantic salmon?**

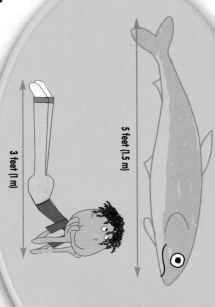

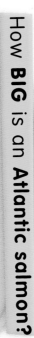

5 feet (1.5 m)

3 feet (1 m)

Salmon eat fish such as herring and pilchards, as well as squid and crustaceans.

After breeding, Atlantic salmon return to the sea. They may breed again a few years later.

Most other types of salmon die after laying or fertilizing their eggs.

Moray Eel

Moray eels live in coral reefs and shallow **coastal** waters of the northern Atlantic Ocean. They like to hide between rocks and launch surprise attacks on their prey.

There are about 100 species of moray eel. They like to eat fish and mollusks such as octopuses.

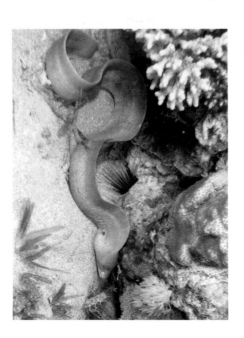

Moray eels have wide mouths. Their many sharp teeth help them hold on to their squirming prey and keep it from escaping.

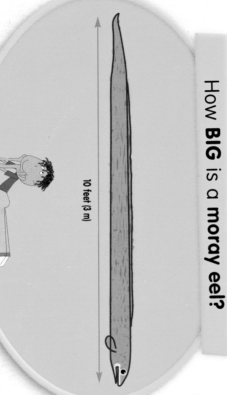

How **BIG** is a **moray eel?**

10 feet (3 m)

3 feet (1 m)

Moray eels are fish, not snakes. They have gills for breathing.

Moray eels do not see well. But that's OK, since they don't have to look for prey. They just wait for it to swim by.

Basking Shark

Basking sharks are found all over the world.

Like other sharks, they are fish. Their name comes from their habit of floating near the water's surface to bask in, or soak up, the sun.

Basking sharks eat **plankton,** small crustaceans, **larvae,** and fish eggs.

See the long, dark **gill slits** in this shark's mouth? They take **oxygen** from the water so the shark can breathe.

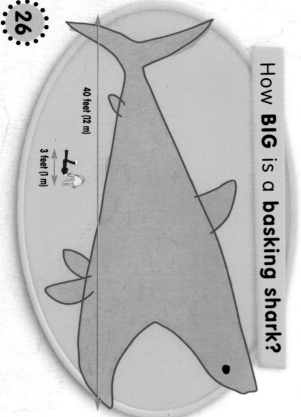

How **BIG** is a **basking shark?**

40 feet (12 m)

3 feet (1 m)

Basking sharks' enormous mouths are filled with hundreds of tiny teeth.

A basking shark feeds by swimming with its mouth wide open. It eats any animals floating in its path.

Hammerhead Shark

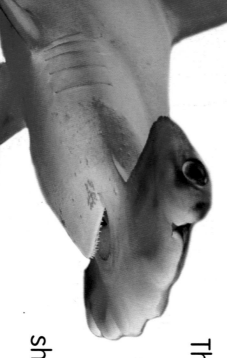

The hammerhead shark's name comes from the strange shape of its head. It looks a lot like a hammer! This shark is found in warm oceans throughout the world.

The eyes and nostrils of the hammerhead shark are at the ends of its head. It has sharp, jagged teeth.

Hammerhead sharks eat squid, octopuses, rays (see page 32), crustaceans, and even other sharks.

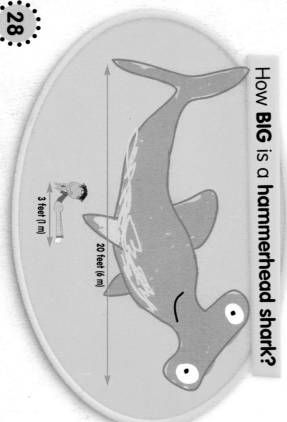

How **BIG** is a **hammerhead shark?**

20 feet (6 m)

3 feet (1 m)

There are five different species of hammerhead shark. All are extremely dangerous.

Female hammerhead sharks give birth to between 20 and 40 live young at a time. Each one is about 27 inches (69 cm) long.

Great White Shark

The great white shark is the most dangerous fish in the sea. It lives in warm, tropical waters.

The great white shark has powerful jaws and rows of sharp teeth. It eats large fish, seabirds, seals, and dolphins.

A great white shark may have as many as 3,000 teeth that measure up to 3 inches (8 cm) long.

How **BIG** is a **great white shark?**

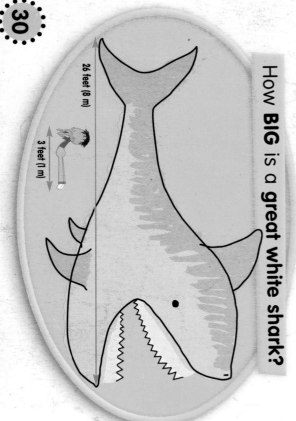

26 feet (8 m)

3 feet (1 m)

The great white shark is built for hunting. It has good eyesight and an excellent sense of smell. In fact, it can smell food or a tiny trace of blood from a long way away.

Manta Ray

The manta ray is a huge fish found in warm oceans.

Its name comes from the Spanish word for blanket, because of its wide, flat fins.

The manta ray can leap up to 5 feet (1.5 m) out of the water. But scientists are not sure why the fish does this. It may be a way to escape a predator or to rid its skin of parasites.

The manta is the largest of more than 300 species of rays.

How **BIG** is a **manta ray?**

20 feet (6 m)

3 feet (1 m)

The manta ray cruises the surface of the water, gathering plankton, small fish, and shellfish to eat. It has special fins on the sides of its head that curl inward to direct food into its mouth.

Manta rays are dark brown or black on top and white underneath.

Parrotfish

Parrotfish live in tropical seas, mainly around coral reefs. It's not hard to see how they got their name. They come in many bright colors and have sharp, beak-like mouths.

Parrotfish use their beaks to scrape algae from rocks and coral. This helps coral reefs stay clean.

If a parrotfish accidentally bites off a piece of coral, the coral gets ground up and passes through the fish's body as sand.

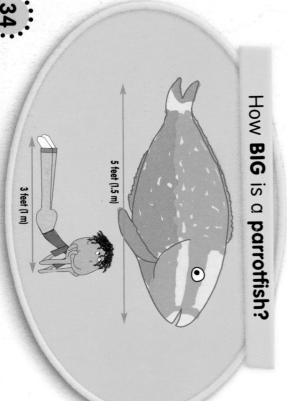

How **BIG** is a **parrotfish?**

5 feet (1.5 m)

3 feet (1 m)

Parrotfish come in many colors, patterns, and sizes. There are about 80 different species.

Seahorse

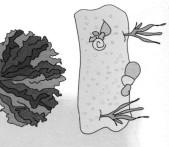

Seahorses are small, bony fish that live in warm water. Their heads are shaped like horses' heads, and they use their curly tails to cling to seaweed.

Seahorses cannot swim fast to keep away from predators. They use **camouflage** instead, changing color to blend in with their surroundings.

A female seahorse lays eggs, then puts them in a pouch on her mate's belly. He will carry them until they hatch.

How **BIG** is a **seahorse?**

6 inches (15 cm)

36 inches (91 cm)

A seahorse uses its long snout to suck up plankton, small shrimp, and fish larvae.

There are 34 different species of seahorses.

Flying Fish

Flying fish live in warm or tropical oceans. They have an amazing skill: they can leap out of the water and glide through the air.

Flying fish hold their fins out like wings as they leap.

Only one species of flying fish actually can fly short distances. The rest just glide on moving air.

How **BIG** is a **flying fish?**

9 inches (24 cm)

36 inches (91 cm)

A flying fish uses its skill to escape from predators. It swims rapidly toward the surface before it shoots out into the air.

Flying fish eat plankton and small crustaceans.

Blue Whale

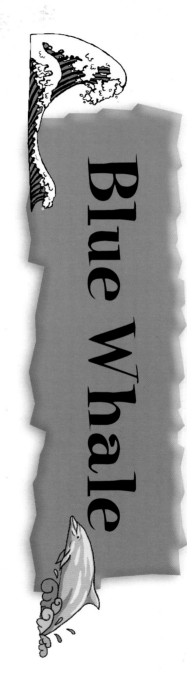

The blue whale is the largest animal in the world. It spends summers in polar seas. It **migrates** to warmer waters during cold months.

The blue whale takes in a mouthful of water then forces it out through its **baleen** plates. Baleen is like a comb that traps **krill**, the whale's main food.

A female blue whale gives birth to one baby every 2 to 3 years. Like all whales, she feeds her young with milk from her body.

How **BIG** is a **blue whale?**

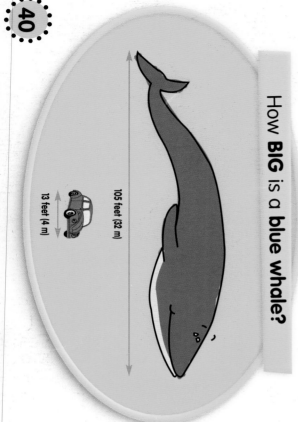

105 feet (32 m)

13 feet (4 m)

Like other whales and human beings, the blue whale breathes using lungs. It blows stale air out through a blowhole in the top of its head.

Humpback Whale

Humpback whales are found in the Arctic, Pacific, and Atlantic Oceans. They migrate between cool waters that are full of food and warmer areas where they raise their young.

Like some other kinds of whales, humpback whales feed by filtering fish and krill through their baleen.

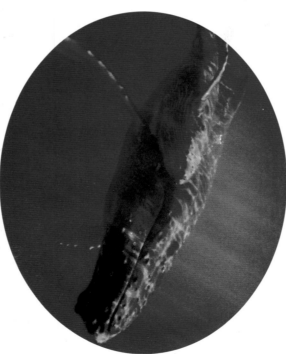

Humpback whales are gray and black with long, narrow flippers.

How **BIG** is a **humpback whale?**

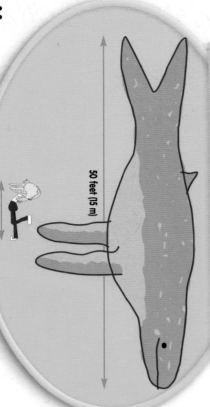

50 feet (15 m)

3 feet (1 m)

Humpback whales like to be with other humpbacks. They leap out of the water and land with a splash, either for play or to attract a mate.

Sperm Whale

The sperm whale is found in oceans all over the world. It is grayish blue with a pale belly. It has tiny flippers and large, powerful tail **flukes**.

Like all whales, the sperm whale has to come to the surface for a breath of air.

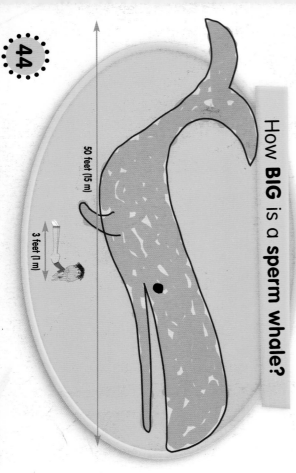

How **BIG** is a **sperm whale?**

50 feet (15 m)

3 feet (1 m)

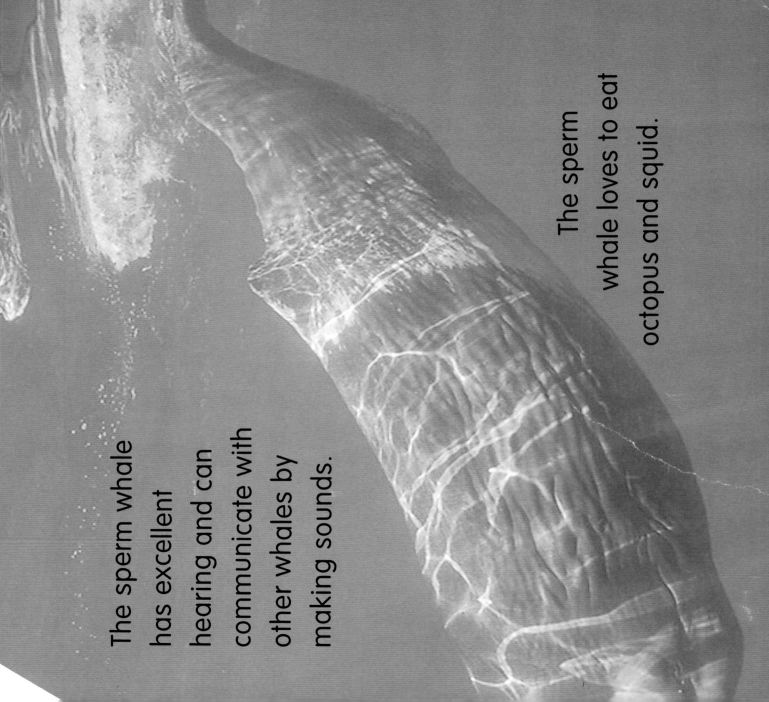

The sperm whale has excellent hearing and can communicate with other whales by making sounds.

The sperm whale loves to eat octopus and squid.

It can dive deep below the surface and stay underwater for more than an hour without coming up for air.

Dolphin

Dolphins are found in oceans all over the world. They look like fish, but they are actually mammals. They give birth to live young.

Dolphins like to live and play together. They use sounds and movements to communicate.

How **BIG** is a bottlenose dolphin?

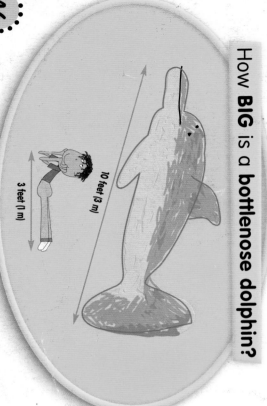

10 feet (3 m)

3 feet (1 m)

There are more than 30 kinds of dolphins. The bottlenose dolphin is popular at zoos and aquariums.

Dolphins have small, sharp teeth for eating fish. Their flippers and long **dorsal fin** make them fast swimmers and great jumpers.

Orca

Orcas are found in oceans all over the world, but they prefer colder seas over warmer waters. They are mammals, and the largest type of dolphin.

Orcas are often called killer whales. They are not really whales, but they are expert hunters.

How **BIG** is an **orca?**

25 feet (7.5 m)

3 feet (1 m)

The orca's black and white coloring and tall dorsal fin make it easy to recognize.

Like other dolphins, orcas like to live in groups called pods.

The orca eats fish, squid, and seals, as well as larger animals like porpoises and small sharks.

Manatee

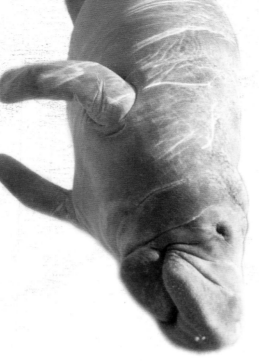

Manatees are mammals that live in coastal areas of West Africa and North and South America. There are three species of manatees.

A manatee's nostrils are high on its snout so it can breathe even when most of its body is underwater.

They can stay underwater for about 20 minutes at a time.

How **BIG** is a manatee?

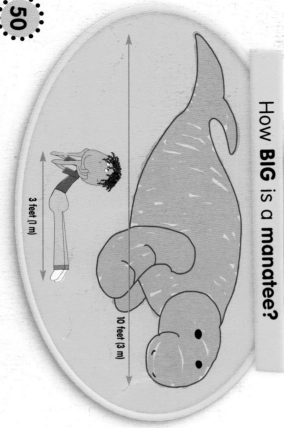

3 feet (1 m)

10 feet (3 m)

A manatee moves very slowly. It has two paddle-shaped flippers and a flat tail.

Manatees spend all their lives in the water. They sleep with their nostrils above the surface so they can breathe.

Sea Otter

The sea otter is an ocean mammal that is related to the weasel. It lives off the coast of the United States in the northern Pacific Ocean.

Sea otters eat clams and other mollusks. They sometimes use a rock to smash open the shells. They also eat fish and crabs.

Unlike most ocean mammals, sea otters don't have a fat layer called **blubber** to keep them warm. They do have thick, waterproof fur.

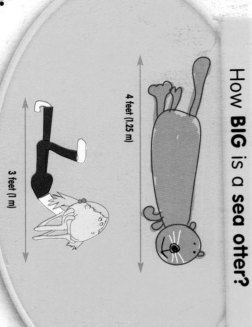

How **BIG** is a **sea otter**?

4 feet (1.25 m)

3 feet (1 m)

Sea otters swim on their backs. They have up to 800 million hairs on their bodies, which trap air and help to keep them afloat.

Sea otters breed throughout the year and give birth to one pup at a time.

53

Harp Seal

Harp seals have sleek bodies that are perfect for swimming in the icy waters of the Arctic. They get their name from a black patch of fur on their backs that is shaped like a harp.

Baby harp seals have pure white fur. This helps them blend in with ice and snow.

Harp seals catch and eat fish and crustaceans.

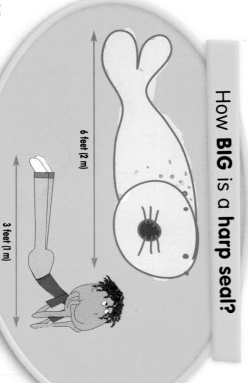

How **BIG** is a **harp seal**?

6 feet (2 m)

3 feet (1 m)

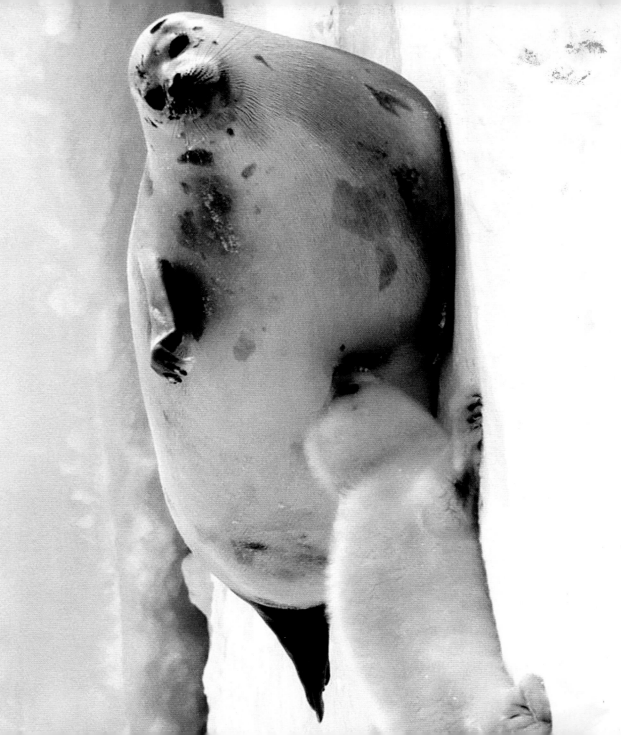

Adult harp seals have short, thick coats that are gray with black patches. A thick layer of blubber under their skin keeps them warm.

Harp seals spend most of their lives in the water. They come ashore to mate and give birth to their pups. This pup is having a drink of milk.

Walrus

The walrus is a large mammal that is related to the seal. It lives in the waters of the Arctic and is covered in thick blubber to protect it from the cold.

Walruses sleep in the water and have air-filled sacs on the sides of their necks that help to keep them afloat.

A walrus mother is very protective of her pup. She may also adopt a pup whose mother has died.

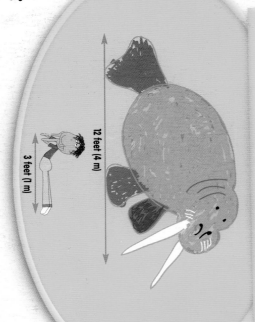

How **BIG** is a **walrus?**

12 feet (4 m)

3 feet (1 m)

Walruses like to lie in large groups on the ice. Males and females meet up only at mating time.

The walrus with the biggest **tusks** holds the most important place in his or her group.

Penguin

Penguins are birds that can swim very well, but do not fly. There are 17 species that live along ocean shores in the southern half of the world.

Penguins spend most of their time in the water catching fish, krill, and squid to eat. Their wings work like flippers.

During the warmer months, emperor penguins gather on the ice of Antarctica to breed.

How **BIG** is a **penguin?**

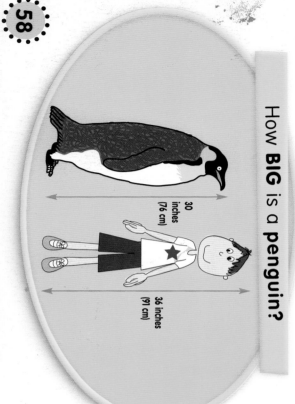

30 inches (76 cm)

36 inches (91 cm)

These emperor penguins are built to survive the cold. They have thousands of tiny feathers and a layer of fat under their skin for warmth.

Most penguins live in places where the weather is not too cold or too hot.

Banded Sea Snake

The banded sea snake lives in all the world's oceans except the Atlantic. It shoots venom into its prey when it bites.

The tail end of a banded sea snake's body is flat, which helps it to swim fast.

This reptile gives birth to live young underwater.

Banded sea snakes never leave the water, but they come to the surface to breathe.

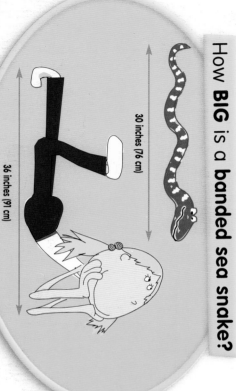

How **BIG** is a **banded sea snake?**

30 inches (76 cm)

36 inches (91 cm)

Banded sea snakes eat crabs, cuttlefish, eels, fish, fish eggs, and squid.

Saltwater Crocodile

The saltwater crocodile is the largest reptile on the planet. Other kinds of crocodiles live in rivers, but these fierce beasts feel right at home in salty coastal waters near Australia, Indonesia, and Asia.

The saltwater crocodile spends most of its life hiding in the water, waiting for its next victim to wander by.

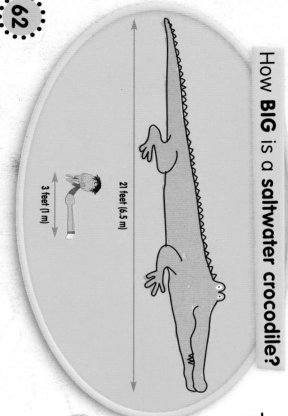

How **BIG** is a **saltwater crocodile?**

21 feet (6.5 m)

3 feet (1 m)

A saltwater crocodile moves with astonishing speed, dragging its victim down and tearing off large chunks of flesh.

It eats crustaceans, fish, turtles, and birds. Sometimes it eats larger animals, such as buffalo.

Green Turtle

The green turtle lives in warm, coastal waters of the Atlantic. It gets its name from the green color of its fat.

The green turtle comes to land when it wants to warm up in the sunlight or sleep.

The female green turtle digs a hole in the sand and lays her eggs. Then she returns to the water.

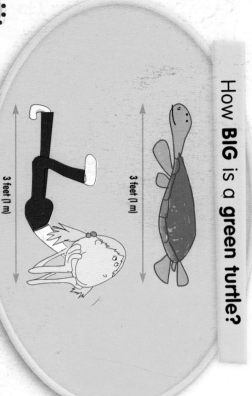

How **BIG** is a **green turtle**?

3 feet (1 m)

3 feet (1 m)

The green turtle travels long distances to lay its eggs on beaches in Central America and the Caribbean Sea. The Galapagos Islands are a favorite nesting place.

Leatherback Turtle

The leatherback turtle is found in oceans all over the world. It gets its name because its shell is made up of ridges of bone with a bendy leathery covering.

Like all turtles, the leatherback turtle comes ashore to lay its eggs. When the baby turtles hatch, they hurry to the safety of the water.

The leatherback turtle is the largest of all turtles.

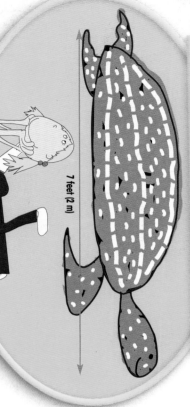

How **BIG** is a **leatherback turtle?**

7 feet (2 m)

3 feet (1 m)

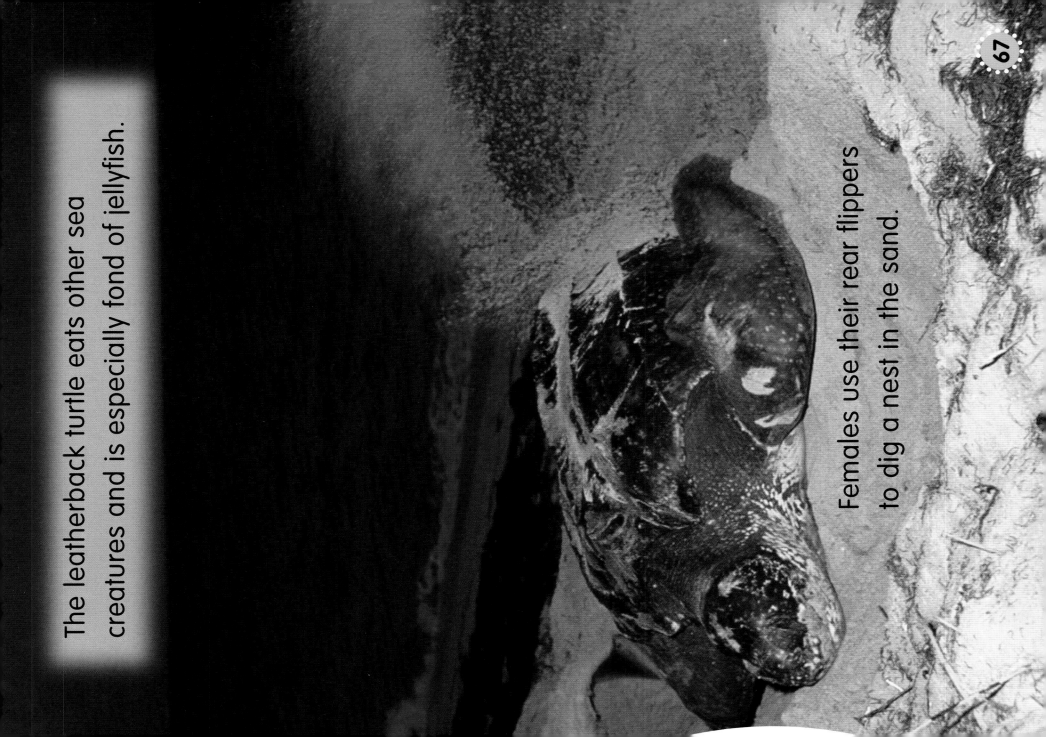

The leatherback turtle eats other sea creatures and is especially fond of jellyfish.

Females use their rear flippers to dig a nest in the sand.

Marine Iguana

Marine iguanas are a type of lizard. They live on the Galapagos Islands, which lie off the west coast of South America. They eat algae off rocks along the shore.

Marine iguanas can remain underwater for up to an hour. Usually they surface every 5 to 10 minutes to breathe.

Females are not very colorful. Males may have red and green patches on their backs.

How **BIG** is a marine iguana?

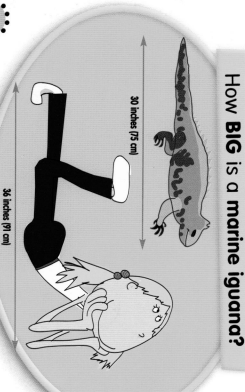

30 inches (75 cm)

36 inches (91 cm)

When males fight, they use their heads to try and push each other backward. The loser has to go away.

Fiddler Crab

Fiddler crabs are tiny crustaceans. They live on beaches in warm and tropical parts of the world. They dig deep burrows in the sand for shelter.

Male fiddler crabs have one large claw that may be as big as the rest of its body. In females, both claws are small.

Fiddler crabs use a small claw to scoop sand into their mouths. They sift out algae and other food and spit out the sand that is left.

How **BIG** is a **fiddler crab?**

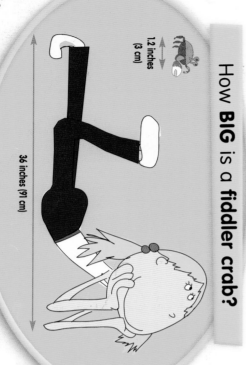

1.2 inches (3 cm)

36 inches (91 cm)

Males look as if they are playing a fiddle, or violin (the large claw), when they use the small claw to eat.

Hermit Crab

The soft-bodied hermit crab is found in oceans all over the world. It uses another animal's empty shell as its home and carries it wherever it goes.

The eyes of a hermit crab are on the ends of stalks that stick out of its head.

Hermit crabs have ten jointed legs. The two front legs have pincers, or claws.

How **BIG** is a **hermit crab?**

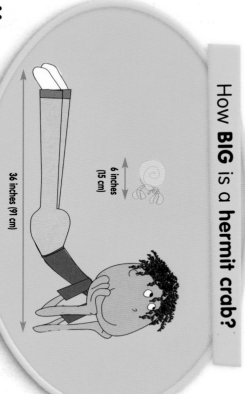

6 inches (15 cm)

36 inches (91 cm)

When a hermit crab grows out of the shell it is using, it just finds a bigger one.

Hermit crabs are **scavengers** that eat anything they can find, including plants, plankton, and even dead sea creatures.

Mantis Shrimp

Mantis shrimp are small but fierce crustaceans that live in the coastal waters of tropical and warm oceans. Despite their name, they are not related to shrimp.

Mantis shrimp kill their prey by hitting the victim with their powerful, club-like front legs.

Mantis shrimp eat fish. Some of these fish may be much larger than the mantis shrimp!

How **BIG** is a **mantis shrimp?**

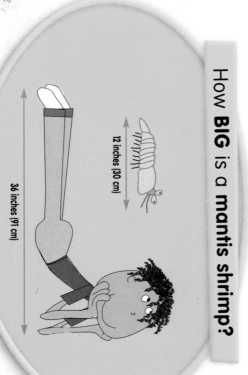

12 inches (30 cm)

36 inches (91 cm)

Mantis shrimp can strike with amazing force. They can even break safety glass in aquarium walls.

Lobster

Lobsters are crustaceans that live in oceans all over the world. They begin their life as tiny floating creatures that make up plankton.

The lobster is protected by a hard **exoskeleton** on the outside of its body.

Lobsters grow throughout their lives. They shed their old exoskeleton, and a new, larger one grows in its place.

How **BIG** is a **lobster?**

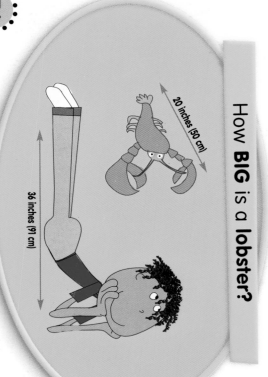

20 inches (50 cm)

36 inches (91 cm)

Lobsters have five pairs of jointed legs. The front ones have large, powerful claws that are used for crushing prey.

Lobsters are scavengers and will eat whatever they find, but shellfish are a favorite. They may also attack live fish.

Octopus

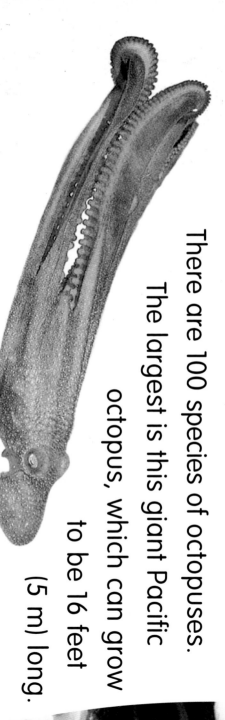

Octopuses have eight tentacles, or arms, that are covered in suckers. They use these to catch fish and crustaceans to eat.

There are 100 species of octopuses. The largest is this giant Pacific octopus, which can grow to be 16 feet (5 m) long.

There are two different kinds of blue-ringed octopuses. Both of them have a bite that delivers deadly venom.

How **BIG** is a **blue-ringed octopus?**

4 inches (10 cm)

36 inches (91 cm)

The blue-ringed octopus is found in shallow pools off the coast of Australia. When resting, it is pale brown or yellow. It shows its blue rings only when it senses danger.

In order to escape danger, octopuses squirt a black, inky liquid into the water so it's hard for a predator to see. Then they swim away.

Jellyfish

Jellyfish live in oceans all over the world. They have soft bodies and long, stinging tentacles, which they use to catch fish. There are 215 different species of jellyfish.

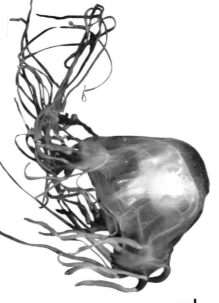

The box jellyfish's coloring makes it hard to see, even in clear water.

How BIG is a box jellyfish?

6.5 feet (2 m)

3 feet (1 m)

The sting of the box jellyfish can be deadly.

This is a cannonball jellyfish.

A jellyfish's mouth is on the underside of its body, in the middle of the tentacles.

Squid

Squid are a group of mollusks that live in oceans all over the world. They are closely related to the octopus.

Squid eat fish, crustaceans, and other squid. When they are angry or frightened, they can change color to blend in with their surroundings.

Giant squid can reach 50 feet (15 m) in length. They are very rare.

How BIG is a giant squid?

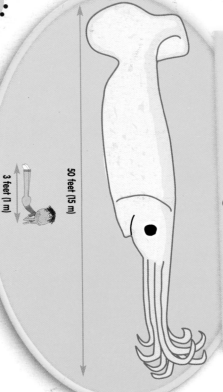

50 feet (15 m)

3 feet (1 m)

The squid can squirt a dark liquid called ink to make the water cloudy.

Squid have two long tentacles and eight shorter arms. They have a long body with two triangular fins at the end.

Oyster

Oysters are mollusks that are prized for the pearls they produce. There are many different varieties, and they are found in every ocean.

If a piece of sand enters its shell, the oyster coats the sand with a shiny substance called nacre to keep it from scratching. This makes a pearl.

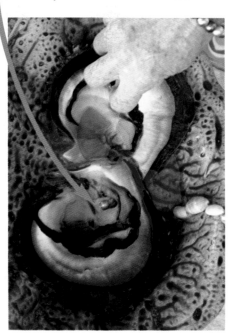

An oyster's shell has two halves that it holds tightly closed. This hard covering protects the soft body of the oyster.

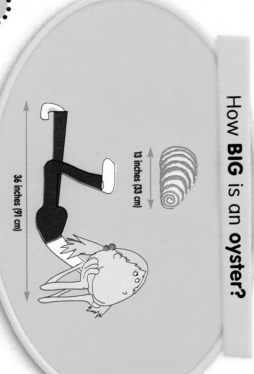

How **BIG** is an **oyster?**

13 inches (33 cm)

36 inches (91 cm)

Oysters draw in water through their gills. The water provides oxygen for breathing and algae for food.

Oysters cluster in groups called beds. They often attach themselves to rocks.

Coral

Coral may look like a plant, but it is actually made up of tiny, soft-bodied invertebrates called polyps. They live in oceans around the world.

Coral polyps fasten themselves to other polyps or to the seabed to form a group called a colony. Coral can be many shapes and colors.

Many coral polyps make a substance that forms a hard skeleton around their bodies. These skeletons remain on the seabed even after the polyps die.

How **BIG** is a **coral?**

one polyp is very tiny, but a colony can grow very large

3 feet (1 m)

Coral polyps cannot move. They use tentacles that surround their mouths to collect plankton from the water.

Sea Anemone

Sea anemones (ah-NEM-o-nees) look like flowers, but they are meat-eating animals. They are found all over the world in deep oceans, coastal waters, and shallow areas such as coral reefs.

The sea anemone lives its life attached to the ocean floor, but it can move very slowly.

Sea anemones eat small crustaceans, fish, and mussels, which they sting with their poisonous tentacles.

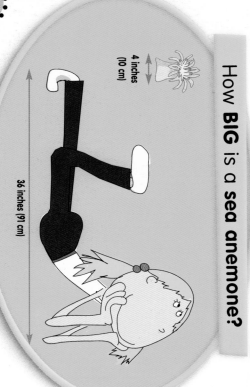

How **BIG** is a **sea anemone?**

4 inches (10 cm)

36 inches (91 cm)

The body of a sea anemone is shaped like a tube. The mouth is at the top, surrounded by stinging tentacles.

There are more than 1,000 kinds of sea anemones.

Sea Cucumber

The sea cucumber is an invertebrate that looks like a giant worm. It is found in oceans all over the world, from tropical waters to colder areas.

They have spiny skin, which makes it hard for predators to eat them.

Sea cucumbers eat plankton that they filter from the water or the sand.

How **BIG** is a **sea cucumber**?

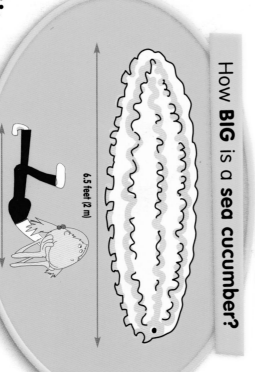

6.5 feet (2 m)

3 feet (1 m)

Sea cucumbers have five rows of tube feet with tiny suction cups. These are used to crawl along the seabed or hold on to rocks.

A sea cucumber is one of the most basic forms of life. It does not even have a brain.

The mouth of the sea cucumber is surrounded by between 8 and 30 tentacles.

Starfish

Starfish are not really fish. They are invertebrates. They are found in oceans all over the world and live in shallow water near beaches. They are also called sea stars.

Starfish have at least five arms, or tentacles. They use rows of suckers on the tentacles to pull themselves along.

A starfish has hard, bony plates under its skin called ossicles that protect its soft body.

How **BIG** is a **starfish?**

8 inches (20 cm)

36 inches (91 cm)

Starfish use their tentacles to open the shells of oysters and other mollusks. With their mouths, they suck up the food inside.

There are 1,500 known species of starfish in a wide range of sizes.

Glossary

algae: plant-like living things that do not produce seeds or flowers. Seaweed is a kind of algae.

baleen: thin strands of keratin (what fingernails are made of) that hang in sheets or plates from the upper jaw of some whales. They are used to filter food from the water.

blubber: a layer of fat under the skin of some animals that protects them from the cold

breed: to come together for the purpose of mating and giving birth to young

camouflage: the ability to hide by blending in with the colors and patterns of one's surroundings

coastal: relating to the area where land and an ocean come together

crustaceans: members of a group of mostly water animals with jointed legs and a hard shell. Crabs, lobsters, and shrimp are crustaceans.

dorsal fin: a thin, often pointy body part on the top of a fish or a dolphin

estuary: an area where a freshwater river meets the salty ocean

exoskeleton: the hard outer covering of an animal or insect that supports or protects its soft insides

extinct: no longer existing on earth

fertilize: to add a substance from one's body to eggs so that the eggs will develop into young. A male fish must fertilize a female's eggs for them to hatch.

flukes: the flat sections of a whale's tail

fry: young fish

gill slits: openings in the sides of fish and some other ocean animals. Water flows in through the slits and passes over the gills, allowing the animal to breathe.

gills: a body part in fish and some other ocean animals that allows them to breathe underwater

invertebrates: animals that have no backbone, or spine. Invertebrates include mollusks, crustaceans, spiders, insects, and worms.

krill: tiny, shrimp-like ocean creatures that are eaten by whales and other creatures

larvae: the name for the young of some animals that are in a stage of life between egg and adult

mammals: animals with hair or fur that give birth to live babies and feed them with their own milk

migrate: to travel long distances on a regular schedule

mollusks: a group of invertebrate animals with soft, segmented bodies, usually protected by a shell. Snails, clams, squid, and octopuses are mollusks.

oxygen: a chemical found in air and water that is necessary for life

parasite: an animal that feeds on another animal without killing it

plankton: tiny animals and plants that float and drift in open water and are a source of food for other water animals

predator: an animal that eats other animals

prey: an animal that is food for other animals

reflect: to send back light like a mirror

reptiles: a group of animals that includes snakes, lizards, tortoises, and turtles. Reptiles are cold-blooded (their body temperature matches their surroundings), and they have scaly skin.

scales: small, stiff pieces of skin that cover the bodies of fish and reptiles

scavenger: an animal that feeds off whatever dead animals and leftovers it can find, rather than hunting for itself

seabed: the bottom of the ocean

species: one specific kind of animal, such as the bottlenose dolphin

tentacle: a long, flexible organ used for holding, feeling, or moving

tropical: relating to certain hot parts of the world near the equator

tusks: long, sharp teeth, usually grown in pairs and often used for digging and fighting

venom: poison that flows from an animal's mouth parts. Venom is used to paralyze or kill other animals for food.

vertebrates: animals that have a backbone, or spine. Vertebrates include fish, mammals, birds, reptiles, and amphibians.

Index